In memory of Mom and Dad,
Lillian R. and Arthur L. Smith, Sr.,
with all my love

Muriel E. Vetsky

Copyright © 2013 by Muriel E. Vebsky
First Edition – March 2013

ISBN
978-1-4602-0706-2 (Hardcover)
978-1-4602-0704-8 (Paperback)
978-1-4602-0705-5 (eBook)

All rights reserved.

No part of this publication may be reproduced in any form, or by any means, electronic or mechanical, including photocopying, recording, or any information browsing, storage, or retrieval system, without permission in writing from the publisher.

Produced by:

FriesenPress
Suite 300 – 852 Fort Street
Victoria, BC, Canada V8W 1H8

www.friesenpress.com

Distributed to the trade by The Ingram Book Company

Bear With Me

Would to God you could bear
      With me a little,
As I present a means
      Of showing love.
From deep within my soul
      A rhythm strung
As unforsaken thoughts
      Of ideas come.

My thanks to Terry Fisher for her many hours of work typing on the computer and talking on the telephone to complete this poetry book.

LISTENING
and other poems

BY MURIEL E. VEBSKY

CONTENTS

Bear With Me	iii
Listening	1
Another Season	2
More Than Gold	3
Miracles	3
Jewels of Winter	4
No Nesting	5
Value of Life	5
Warmth	6
Star Dust	6
The Day We Die	7
Path of Love	7
Rescue	8
Icy Splendor	9
White Forest	9
A Bird's Song	10
Power of Death	11
Bouyant Joy	12
I Can See	13
Nostalgia	15
Pausing of a Shadow	16
Indian Summer	16
Bird's Song	17
Spring Comes Forth	18
Changing of Time	19
Hear	19

CONTENTS / *continued* /

Inward Sigh	20
Head Held High	20
Worthy as Trout	21
Quiet Satisfaction	23
This Old Oak	24
Fall	24
Birch Trees	25
Peace	25
Island Hotel	26
Poignant Moment	27
Feel of Earth	28
Flying Ducks	29
Beauty of Dirt	30
Young Farmer's Dream	31
Arms Outstretched	32
Jesus Alone	32
Smile	33
Luminous Light	34
His Own World	35
Icy Cold	36
Walking in the Pouring Rain	36
Hope	37
In Love We Dwell	38
Enigma Aura	39
Comfortless	41
Time Is Not Come	41

Breath of Life	42
Effects of Love	42
Dexterous Diggings	43
There's A Way	44
There's Room	45
What Should He Do?	45
Come Home	46
The One I Seek	47
Love's Seed	47
Better Things	48
Unspeakable Joy	48
God, Let Me	49
Wonderland of Snow	50
Love	51
Rule For Life	52
In the Whiteness of the Moon	53
Instruction of a Father	54
Trusting His Love	54
Throughout All Life	55
Eyes	56
Tiny Babe	57
Mystery of Life	58
It's Amazing	59
In Front of My Window	60
Tread It Down	61
Reach Out	62

CONTENTS /*continued*/

Affliction	63
The Burden	64
Legends of Miracles	65
Only a Rose	66
My Dad	67
Saved	67
Chasing the Wind	68
No Rejoice	69
When He Looked Round	70
All Ways	71
Hearing	72
Luscious Springtime	73
Height of Hope	74
Rushing Waves	75
Toward Tomorrow	76
Shadows	77
Why?	78
Son Shines	79
Through Dense Darkness	80
A Tear is Shed	81
Feeling Great	82
Life Has Not Lost Its Music	83
The Daughters of the King	84
In the Cookie Jar	85
Troubled Waters	87
Sister	88

It Can't Be Bought	89
Last Lunge	90
That Sinking Feeling!	91
Joy	93
Friendship	94

Listening

I love to sit and listen
To limbs bow in the trees,
There is a lot of whisper'n
Amongst the new formed leaves.
I love to sit and listen
As birds lite in the trees,
They fill the air with singing
To jostle growing leaves.
I love to sit and listen
As rain comes flooding down,
The drops are light and glistening
As wind whips them aroun'.
I love to sit and listen
As the pounding in the trees,
Becomes a band of musicians
Making music with the leaves.
I love to sit and listen
As leaves do talk about
The great huge puddle wavering
In the breeze as it fills out.

Another Season

Sparrows are in a tree near me,
A piece of paper I can see
Them tugging on so viciously.
Soon all but one do fly away,
Then that tiny little mite
Grabs the paper with one bite.
Off he flies to give his mate,
Whose nesting ever by the lake
His offering that is first rate.
She picks it up in her short beak,
Pushes it gently with her feet,
Looks at him with a sly wink.
Birds sing cheerfully with reason,
For paper leaves on trees are pleasin'
As spring begins another season.

More Than Gold

Christ walks the earth, removing all sorrow,
Stumbling and falling, I try to follow.
My steps stray from His
Then voice heavy with tears
He calls, "Follow me, I'll carry more load,
I love you, I'll give you much more than gold'
My head hangs low as my steps follow His.
The greatest burden I now have
Is causing Christ's tears.

Miracles

Lasting friendships such as ours
Are miracles of our Heavenly Father
Filling each heart He holds as precious
True love for mankind He asks us.

Jewels of Winter

Diamonds glisten over the ground
    Upon the top of the snow,
        That fell through the night
            And woke with a glow.
Dancing and prancing are the dots
    Shimmering in the sunshine,
        Warming the hearts of everyone,
            Even those who haven't a dime.
Feast your eyes on the trillions
    Of tiny specks of hope,
        That come from every place
            Where people do not mope.
Brightness shines over the earth
    All blanketed in white,
        So clean from its washing
            During the night.

No Nesting

Birds do bicker noisily
Trying a bit of paper to free
As breezes wave it huskily
And wrap it more securely
Round the leaves of a small tree
Where a nesting place it refused to be.

Value of Life

Oh, Lord, I know I'm not worthy to be,
Constructing a poem or song to Thee.
Deep in my soul Thy Spirit inspires
Words that come are like burning fires.
The salt of the earth, the light of the world,
Depend upon me, how I carry my load.
Love relatives, friends, strangers, too,
Pray, give presents, don't bend the rule
Forgive and forget when harm befalls,
Value each life, for God made us all.

Warmth

The spirit of the mind is lost
    when nothing is found
        beyond to hold.
A sense of cosmic loneness
    inwardly sparkles
        void and cold.
Love of friends returns the joy
    so life resumes
        it's music bold.

Star Dust

I look at the moonlit heaven
Listen to the wind sweep past,
All around the stars are falling
Sprinkling dust so thick and fast.

The Day We Die

Only God knows the reason why
We live until the day we die.
The spirit of the mind is lost
When nothing lifts our eyes aloft.
If only we had known He cared
Dignity of each soul be bared,
The Son of God gave up His life
His silent struggle captured strife,
Yet the rush of troubled waters fled
When Jesus Christ smiled down and said.
'Trust in Me, My Love and Grace,
To see beyond to our Father's place'.

Path of Love

Tender the path of love so true.
Since first my eyes caught sight of you,
Fair as a drop from the honeycomb,
With you I'll never again be alone,
Sweet as the blossom of the apple tree,
As long as you give your love to me.

Rescue

The mountainous area is filled with caves
    which shelter wolves.
Straying sheep seek thickets for food
    along false paths,
Tis death o're a sharp precipice
    either way devoured,
Life can't spare difficult experiences
    regardless of level,
Promise is the recourse of light
    to be tapped,
Walk THROUGH the valley of death
    fear no evil.
Use the staff to prevent the feared fall
    into dark depths,
Take the Almighty along pathways of life
    for security flowing,
Abiding presence of God is continuous help
    beyond all knowing.

Icy Splendor

On a wonderfully clear crisp day
In its majestic massive existence,
Snow-covered and misty white,
The mountain looms in the distance.
Around the fog-filled bay spectacular
Seals sun themselves on opaque floes,
As ice burgs, glaciers, and other wild life
Rise in splendor of natural noise.

White Forest

Snow, blow into every empty space
Cover the trees with delicate lace.
Heavy branches in slow pace
Bow wintry forest, to His grace.

A Bird's Song

One morning I was feeling sad
      Which wasn't meant to be,
For next to me I heard a song
      As sweet as it could be.
A red-winged blackbird in a tree
      Surrounding beauty he did see.
How can one as big as me
      I am over twenty-three,
Forget that God is here with me
      Sitting 'neath this apple tree,
And the little bird so happy
      Sitting by himself so raptly.

Power of Death

Wisdom guarded to the end
      the first formed father of
           all men.
Strength possessed him totally
      to uplift alone the world
           to be.
Unrighteousness took him and her
      when wifely wiles wherewith
           did err.
Forgiveness in melodious breath
      pursued and paralyzed the power
           of death.

Bouyant Joy

Momentarily
shaken by
angry words of
undeniable pride, yet equally
torn in feelings and belief.

Fear
of rueful
countenance bleak and
terrible loneliness tend to
pierce a weak and ravished soul.

Flourishes
of love
and laughter lightly
take away the thorns
to build bubbling buoyant joy.

I Can See

I can see
God smile upon:
>A warming orange sunrise,
>The tumult of purple thunder clouds,
>Budding shrubs and trees in spring,
>Falling snow that blankets things
>In winter with its cold and ice.
>At babies born,
>Children full of hope and glee,
>Women cleaning house,
>Men when they embrace the home
>With love in deeds and gentle words.

There is no place that God can't see
Something beautiful and fine
Except—
I can see
God frown upon:
>Hasty words when under pressure,
>Brutal acts of hate and anger,
>Disobedient children torn with rejection,
>Cruel sneers from those more fortunate,
>Prejudice with suspicion and intolerance,
>Hurt grown deep within the soul
>Not released with a smile of forgiveness,
>Recklessness, haste, desire of
>What other people possess,
>Lack of heart when grief is great,
>Need of all the old and young
>For their place under God's warm sun.

He put us here to do His will,
Why can't we pray and listen
To the perfect plan already formed?
If we could only BE like Him,
Instead, we try so hard to destroy
All that we can see.
Yet—
I can see
God loves us still.
So He will
Lend a helping hand,
To turn us toward our goal,
If only ALL could see
How beautiful this world could be!

Nostalgia

Nostalgia overwhelms the traveler
   As colors of nature
      Glow in myriad hues.
Early holiday spirit fills the heart
   At the turning
      Of the leaves.
Read maples bright as pyres, puffs of red
   And yellow burst
      From sugar maples.
Brilliant crimson sumacs catch the eye
   Rustling, rustic leaves
      Float slowly, then
As brightness fades to dull browns,
   They swiftly fall in noisy
      Whispers to cover
Everything in shaped and shaded tinsel.

Pausing of a Shadow

Pausing of a shadow brings not the end,
The flower of spring crowns the rose thorn.
Come share the revelry
Leave laughter by the way,
A spark among stubble
Casts off all shadow.
Happy is the eunuch
For goodness is renown,
While the heart beats,
Thoughts traverse the mind.
Traces of cloud chase beams from the sun.

Indian Summer

As the sparkle of October's Indian summer
    gives way to snow filled cloud,
November dims the colorful roadside swatches
    of purple aster and goldenrod.

Bird's Song

A leaf has blown from off a tree
To flutter and fall in haste,
It lands right next to me
So I can see its face.
Once again a leaf is lost
It floats down to the earth,
Where does it land at any cost?
Why near the others berth.
They float next to an ugly thing
Translucent, fat and long,
Wriggling on the dusted wing
A bird has found its song.
The rain comes down in hardened sheet
Away the callers fly in haste.
Under the leaves so thick they meet
To chew upon the wormy taste.

Spring Comes Forth

Ducks head east in new-born spring,
With winter feathers thick and warm,
No sun to shine upon brown coats
For heavy rain-clouds bounce about.
Fragrant spices toss the air,
As buds and greening leaves push out
On bush and trees along the route.
Chipmunks, squirrels, fox do scoot
From holes and dens their food to root.
Toward high noon the hazy sun
Disperses dingy thinning clouds,
While honking loud the ducks sail on.
O're towns and mountains they're borne,
Through soft and gentle winds are shorn.
Till I can see them gleefully
Pass above me out to sea.
In the boat we take up the chase,
To see which of us wins the race.
As spring comes forth to cast its spell
Before the ducks can reach the dell.

Changing of Time

Limbs on the trees bow to and fro,
Flinging confetti leaves about,
Like colored snow flakes
Into the crispy hurried air.
Leaves of orange and rustic alike
Are torn from their branches,
Thrust fast into flight,
Tumbling along frosted ground.
Never to stop in the flurry of air,
Sound swelling higher and wider,
As waves roaring over the sea
Blankets earth in changing of time.

Hear

From quietness of mind, O Lord,
Give me the chance to hear
What people say when speaking,
What needs I feel from fear,
What true advice is given,
From the heart of ones most dear.

Inward Sigh

A brook flowing freely in the night
Gurgling over small stones smoothly
Definitely draws a quiet inward sign,
Though cold, black and foreboding,
It plunges over boulders of quick descent,
Then flows furtively, flexibly forward,
With amazing energy in delicate wistful
Stretches of solid sounding buoyant bubbles.

Head Held High

Silence settles down around
      with head held high.
Summer stretches toward fall
      shoulders bravely square,
Something touching and almost beautiful
      glows with satisfaction,
Sinks into delightful exhaustion
      mindful of responsibility.

Worthy as Trout

The rains came fast and steady
    Day and night, day and night
        For a month.
Roaring threateningly in frenzied rampage
    Undercut banks, toppled trees-crashed
        Into rising streams.
Headwater areas up in the hills
    Became maddenly soaked
        Then slipped away.
Trees became toothpicks floating
    Into logjams of slashing flood force
        Cutting new channels.
Grape vineyards were threatened by streams
    With nonexistent banks, gravel deposits
    Raised their bottoms.
Department of Environmental Conservation
    Promised to take care of the streams
        For the trout.
They were so steeped in enforcing regulations
    Some seemed unable to shift mental gears to
        Urgent human need,
Deepening the trout-stream channel was evil itself
    To true-blue fish and game men regardless of
        Hard-earned livelihood.

People could be at least as worthy as trout
        So after a disastrous flood, help could
                Surely be given.
Death to the paper work, get the machine started
        Sacrifice trout, not just plain 'folk' upon the
                Ecological enthusiasm altar.

Quiet Satisfaction

Efficiently and imaginatively managed
    the day is rare indeed,
        as with keen interest,
            people meet
                and speak
                    cordially.
Enriched enjoyment distinctively volatile
    accentuates new delights,
        mingled with gratitude,
            uniquely delicate
                amid ingenious
                    dignity.
With a smile of quiet satisfaction move on,
Self-confidence and foresight to walk alone.

This Old Oak

Falling through the air distorted,
Coats all withered and aborted,
Turned to yellow, brown and red,
Plummeting right past my head,
Are the leaves of this old oak
Standing on the corner soaked.
Thrashing 'bout in wind and rain
Casting forth as though in pain,
Yet the tree with its deep root
Stands up tall in gray wet suit.
And it shall as years roll past
Bloom again, for trees do last.

Fall

The soft sweet breezes blow
Upon the land in sunlit glow
Hear the rustle of the leaves
Sniff the nectar from the trees.
Flowers in a maze of colors
Sweep across the hills and hollows
Summer's beauty deeply sheared
Fall brings winter hastening near.

Birch Trees

Tall and black against dark sky,
Straightway struts each limb,
As the brisk breeze sweeps on by,
Calling each of them to swim,
Feverish in the storm of white
Flakes so lacey, thin and light.
Stiff and stubbornly each holds
Under the brutal ice and cold,
Till at last the limbs decide
Winter will again subside,
So then tall and straight each is
Till summer sun again appears.

Peace

God's sure soft answer fills my life
His silent caring kills all strife.
Throughout the specter of love to peace
Strong relationships never cease.

Island Hotel

It's easy to like the place with
        splendid tropical scenery of
Jungle roots, slithering snakes
        and lizards.
Refreshing swimming in gentle surf,
        once-a-day service to the mainland.
Leisurely lunches before the tours of
        sterile countryside, then
High cliffs with scaling ladder,
        walk alone on the sand of the beach.
Overlooking the cemetery are beds of
        Polyantha roses, ash trees, beds of
Heather and boxwood. Beauty and great
        dignity on smooth green lawns
Where Japanese roses and burchthornes grow,
        to make life full for all.

Poignant Moment

In a world transfused with enchantment
The sky a crimson field patched with purple clouds,
As silence listens in a conifer-scented air
Before swift currents of unceasing gaiety escape
To bring rain drops down in drowning force.
With a nice sense of dramatic values, the droplets
Find a quiet retreat from the troubled world on a rooftop.
But harsh winds of discontent and unrest blow fury
Till each tiny tear becomes a mass of frozen ice
Hanging thickly down, suspended as a stalactite.
Things are brought to their best by struggle
But an icicle grows slowly fatter, glittering and long,
As secretly but none-the-less ardently the sun
Shines hotly, as cold wind whips whimsically
Till the most poignant moment, when all mingle at the top.
Enigmatic smile slightly touched with pride
Incandescent radiance in a strange mysterious place,
Looked down aloof untouchable yonder on the roof,
Known only in silence, the waiting for what or whom
The sun to warm the icicles back to tears.
Leaving the weariness of the world for peace and quiet
Something fiendishly attractive about neglected ground,
Tiny fragments inhale the beauty of a really smashing
sunset
Treasure of thoughts, emotions, have own permanence
As the glitter and sparkle of cold
slowly fades then disappears.

Feel of Earth

Man could be invincible if he'd keep
Close in contact with the earth.
A plot of grass before him,
Canvas overhead to keep him snug and dry
As he listens to the swish of wind
Through branches which echoes ringing
Of cowbells as they bob around necks
Of pastured bovines, munching lazily nearby
A rushing creek meandering along.
The sense of earth so near in
Campfire smoke, roasting of meat,
Glowing embers in the dark of star-
Filled night, all make inner
Stirrings in the depth of mind.
Uncomplicated life, God's gift to
Man if he would but value,
The patter of raindrops from a passing
Shower, the blowing tent flap in the wind
Disclosing mist in valley's depth at dawn.

Flying Ducks

Through steel gray sky and shrill north wind,
In early morn there came
A flock of ducks in a deep vee.
It was a joyous sight to see.
Voice well-tuned to a deep bass
The leader did give steady pace,
To sight the grasses tall and straight
Beside their carefree crystal lake.
The weary fliers swept the sky,
Wings curved wide
They passed not by
But landed with triumphant cry.

Beauty of Dirt

Look outside at all that dirt!
Is it dirty or has it a pleasant
Pleasing beauty of its own?
Many types of rocks, thousands of years of action
By wind and water to wear and grind
Those grains of matter into sand.
Vast deserts have many magnificent moods,
Quiet mystery surrounds with fascination
Stark landscapes of symmetrical mounds of dirt.
Seashore's children saunter, skip, run
Through washed white silvery pearl pebbles
As castles springy and saturated slip into the sea.
Nimble fingers sift soft black dirt into pots
So roots dug deep into the richness of the soil
Jauntily push up flowers of sassy sweetness.
Natural earth glimmers in the sun along
Hard-packed golden dirt roads stretching
Forth in country scenic splendor.
Smell the tormenting musty cleanness as
The plow penetrates the dirt to turn the fields
Clumps of dirt cling to freshly pulled carrots, beets.
What a dull, drab, dreary world indeed
To live without knowing the overwhelming
Beauty of clean, useful, dependable dirt.

Young Farmer's Dream

Amidst bright beauty and tranquility
Mountains and meadows lie still,
Insulated from turbulence of the sea.
Magnificent stands of silvery pine,
In the valley below the red and white farm,
Surround a cluster of rooting swine.
Roosters strut around the barn,
Heralding several hen's brown chicks
Scratching saucily in cracked corn.
Marigolds bloom in an old flower bed,
Zinnias, violets, petunias, and wildroot
Snuggle against a long water shed.
Lazy cows in rock-ordered meadows,
White-heads calmly chewing their cuds,
Watch their frisky calves small shadows.
Morgans saddled near a shallow stream
Wait for barefoot children fishing
Surely every young farmer's dream.

Arms Outstretched

A vision leaped into my head
It was of Christ as He lay dead.
His face so marked in agony
Suffering cruelly on that tree.
For my sins did Jesus die
Yet life eternal now have I.
With arms outstretched God gathers in
Jesus and all who care for Him.

Jesus Alone

Jesus was nailed to that Golgatha tree
His side was pierced with a sharp spear,
Cruel crown of thorns plaited His head
In rejection and denial His followers fled.
Jesus alone in this universe
Conquered sickness, death and disease
At that awesome moment God stepped in
To declare He'd forgiven our sins.

Smile

If solemn the face
        And dull the eye
Of a person you happen to meet,
        Just look at him and wink.
Then part your lips
        In a cheerful smile.
See if that changes
        The looks of him
To a glint in the eye,
        And a thankful grin.

Luminous Light

Into the richness of God's golden earth
Each seed of life is placed,
To bountifully bloom into luminous light,
With the Son for continuous life.
As warm mist rises from cooling ponds
In sprays of spacious vapor clouds,
So life's soul sails smoothly toward
Our humble waiting compassionate Lord.

His Own World

Footsteps thrum in heavy boots
        As he trudges out the door,
Down the broken wooden steps
        To throw a log upon the fire.
It's not the only fire he's made,
        One burns within my heart,
Soaring high into my brain
        Wishing for an early quench
To ease the awful pain
        In my Soul. For why does he
Start and never finish any of his
        Skills? Instead he dreams them
To completion and prays for God
        To still the hammering in his head
And change the world he himself has made.

Icy Cold

The sky is cloudless
The air is still.
Brightness glistens on the snow,
Icy cold bites fingertips,
Toes twinkly in socks for warmth.
The heart beats slowly
As the hurt inside seeps deep.
There is no love to eat away
Sorrow that burns within
The soul of me who has
No tearless eyes to see
The brightness of the world
Through cloudless skies.

Walking in the Pouring Rain

Tripping over rocks across the stream
pipe scented air wafted about them.
Gulls screamed at each other as they soar
over the rolling white caps.
Nook and crannies filled with foamy water.

Hope

Wrath quickly slaughter foolish men,
Envy slowly slays the senseless ones.
He who gives the rain its power
Causes crafty men to failure,
And darkness in their daylight hour.
Let the whirlwinds of desperation
Become warm refreshing hope.
You must eject soul's useless fear
Build confidence and pride
Through love, so peace and quiet can appear.

In Love We Dwell

Contrary winds howl as we throw in the towel
Most of strife in the void of life
Will be conquered if pride is abated.
Passions of hatred cease when hope is released
Strong friendships swell as in love we dwell.

Enigma Aura

Blemishes in the distance
      Though never wholly obliterated,
Seem perpetually intensified
      By sunshine in the corners.
Sky a crimson field patched
      With purple clouds accentuates,
Conifer-scented air mixed
      With innumerable substances.
Unprecedented behavior delicately
      But definitely goes on.
Labor of living, pleasure of work
      Plunge in desperate spasms.
Imperceptible changes occur
      While whole regions bind together,
As crudeness and harshness pour down
      Constantly with fury.
Unwise judgment looks immortal traces
      Of weakness and misery,
Impulsively, thoughtlessly, somewhat
      Reluctantly thrust aside,
Mountains without trees, harsh barren hills,
      Dry river beds,
Elucidate a world transfused
      From disenchantment.
Crisp yellow winter sun
      Bursts brightly overhead,

Snowy cloud galleons sail majestically
        Forward magnified strangely,
Seen through a fish net
        The corners slowly lighten,
Greening hills, colored leaves,
        Esthetic blue horizons,
Valleys of foaming gray
        Are swept safely past,
To make the distance dazzling
        And durable at last.

Comfortless

Rain from bright clouds,
Showers for every blade of grass,
Vanity of false dreams,
Beauty cut asunder as we
Break the bond of brotherhood.
Instrument of those less foolish
Heal the claws of evil.
Woe to the utterly darkened eye.

Time Is Not Come

Consider your ways.
Do you look for much and see little?
Is the beauty around you as of nothing?
The law is tread on by evil.
Work of the heart and hands is for self.
So the mildew and hail is on lost labors.
Destroy the strength of the unlawful
Then only will the time come.

Breath of Life

As the silence swells serene,
    Against the blackest sky,
        Snowflakes softly settle,
So a billowing blanket builds,
    While definite dampness dwindles,
        From the warming breath of life.
Wretched winter winds awaken,
    Thrashing, turbulent, tormenting,
        Disrupted hopes demolished.
For the human race forgets,
    And denies the Lord who,
        Can lift the blackest skies.

Effects of Love

Great and precious, promised blessings
    pivotal though they be
gelid feelings are thrust aside
    to warm and mesmerize
pervasive effects of love
    for perfect harmony.

Dexterous Diggings

While dexterously digging a fox from his burrow
A farmer discovered an antique Indian burial.
Stone implements lay on a mass of red ochre,
On the western shore of a lake in Dakota.
At the head of Frenchmen's Bay perfectly safe until,
The second burial place was found
on a sandy slope of hill.
In a high bluff at Union River's eastern bank,
Another burial was found when sand and gravel sank.
Undisturbed graves held implements in red ochre buried,
Fragments of occipital bone preserved by copper beaded.
There were long spear points made of compact slate,
Pieces of birch-bark upon which bodies were placed.
Implements in ochre from various depths laid,
Chipped knife, pendant, sharpening stone, celt-like blade.
A small chisel, hammerstone with upper part abused,
But blades all polished and cutting edges ready for use.
Indian Point at Bucksport claims an ancient burial place,
At Orland is a gravel knoll-glacial formation space.
Where the ancestry of Eskimo, Red Indian, Algonquin,
Abanaki?
Though the diggings go on, the past stays a mystery.

There's A Way

When hope fills the heart with peace and goodwill
When faith swells the soul till it stretches to God
When love conquers hate then we know there's a way
To lift our burdens throughout every day.
Jesus has asked us to call upon Him
He's more than willing, He already did
Carry our sins to the grave with Him
Then when God lifted His Son for our sake
God and His Son and His Spirit did make
Life on this earth so easy to take.

There's Room

Do you:
> Cling to favorite customs?
> Hold trivia long collected?
> Become intolerant and unlovable?
> Mistake failure in the aged?

Then you:
> Grow stagnant in your lifetime.

So change:
> If you want everlasting joy
> There's room for growth with God.

What Should He Do?

What should he do for you, my child?
Pile you with great possessions,
Take away grief and sadness,
Overcome all persecutors?
Just incline your ear to wisdom,
Apply your heart to understanding,
For wrongdoers shall be cast off
Rooted out of the earth.

Come Home

The heart of the Scottish Highlands
Is a long, long way to come
Bidden, expected, welcomed by none.
No message was sent on ahead
As in desperate search of a quest
Judge, jury nor spectators guess.
I halted in a desolate graveyard
Anxiety, bewilderment spread over face
As that's where my brother was traced.
Why was he killed, what may I ask,
Lay in back of the family tree,
Whilst I was away, to be freed?
Ah, yes – the inheritance galore
Acres of castles, breweries, a stable,
The reason he'd sent me the hurry home cable.

The One I Seek

Have you seen Jesus, He came this way?
I've searched all over night and day.
A gentle man, the One I seek
With voice so soft, calls us His sheep.
He erased our sins from eternity,
Years ago He was nailed to a tree.
He rose from the dead this Son of God,
Heavenly Being, Savior, and Lord.
You must have seen Jesus, He came this way
To comfort and love you every day.
Jesus serene and patient, I seek.
To kneel before Him and wash His feet.

Love's Seed

Help me to see beyond this place,
Uncommon beauty in a plain face.
Let me not walk in circles lost
Trapped by circumstances past.
Courageous enough to undertake
Absolutely devastating time that's late.
Take away passion of hatred and greed,
Fill all broad spaces with love's seed.

Better Things

Better things are yet to come
If you but wait, and watch, and work.
Wait for the joyful happiness,
Watch love fulfilled around you,
Work to lift the load of others
Then comes the better things.
For Jesus Christ gives happiness
From joy you spread around you by
Patience, courage, and silent toil.

Unspeakable Joy

Strangers scatter throughout
Abundant love and lively hope,
Incorruptible undefiled shadows
Fade not away in clouded heavens.
Faith is revealed through seasons
From trial to precious success in
Honor and unspeakable joy.

God, Let Me

God, let me hear Thy Good news
Let me impart Thy word
May others listen as I tell
About Thy Son our Lord.
God, let me be made aware
Of the tasks You have for me
Let me perform them as faithfully
As Jesus saved me on the tree.
God, let me not be the guilty one
Who causes You such pain
Let me instead tell others Lord
Of the life for which Jesus came.

Wonderland of Snow

The sun rises twinkling on icy peaks,
Crimson dawn lights fresh downed snow.
Green mountains and valleys have turned white,
Silent forests bend at the powdery sight.
Bright colored parkas race down the trail,
Red-cheeked and smiling, children sail
Inhaling heavily as breath comes fast,
Eyes alight as winds whip past.
The sport of sailing on seas of snow
Infects all humans young or old.
Snowshoes for the winter walkers
Under branches pace the stalkers.
Alabaster wonderland of snow
Marvels of wintertime brightly unfold,
Trail of a fox, the white of a rabbit,
Night adventures of the deer mouse habit.
A dive in the snow, a skid on the ice,
Love of winter has set humans free
No longer a house-trap for me,
Just hook on some skis and see.
The earth all silver and blue and gold
Magic of skiing can make one bold.
Like the snowflake sailing on high
Sparkle and shout to snow-filled sky.

Love

Day by day, I long to be
      Close to Jesus, so He'll see
How much I need to give to thee
      Love that He has given me.
Be by my side each day, my Lord
      That I will always feel the joys
Your presence in my world unfolds
      While I slip through my household chores.
I have much time to talk to God
      He's within my heart and soul,
So much I need to give to thee
      Love that He has given me.

Rule For Life

Live – with depth and breadth, my friend,
    To realize life while you can.
Love – to break the barriers to others,
    Increase the values beyond yourself.
Learn – to keep the mind alert,
    Be at peace with yourself, be pert.
Think – to understand and know,
    Before you make a wrong decision.
Give – to help and serve and share,
    That other people know you care.
Laugh – or smile, enjoy and play
    With children so they'll grow up fair.
Try – to make a better world,
Show that you are worth more than gold.

In the Whiteness of the Moon

Fruit trees heavy with apples and pears
    Put forth a rich delicious scent.
Huge orange pumpkins, green and yellow squash
    Are visible on frosted leafless vines
        That cover the mountainsides.
Rows of brownish cornstalks stacked
    With gold silken tresses nod in the breeze.
Uncovered in dank freshly dug earth, potatoes
    Tumble from dark beds to lift their eyes
        To the bright clouded skies.
Squirrels chatter as they flit from oak to hazelnut
    As swell cheeked chipmunks stare,
Then scamper into a hollow log nearby
    Hidden under moss and tall tassel grasses,
        Star-filled nights
        are scented, peaceful, cool.
An occasional cricket strums a lonely plaintive
    Tune as insects sing and dance while
Grandfather frog with warty green head, quick thrusting
    Fly catching tongue and a big billowous throat
        Kerchugs in the whiteness of the moon.

Instruction of a Father

Happy is the man that finds wisdom,
By his knowledge the depths are broken up.
Walk in the way of safety, stumble not,
Be not afraid of sudden fear.
Withhold no good from those who need it,
Dwell securely without envy or hate,
Hear the instruction of a father.
We are not amazed at his goodness,
Forthright, quiet, and loving, too.
He takes us by the hand; lifts us up
Cause he knows it's the thing to do.

Trusting His Love

I live each moment trusting His love
Live triumphantly, love embrace,
Freedom, happiness and grace
Being bound to others needs
By caring for my neighbor, too,
By fullness of the deeds I do,
Thank You, God, for joy, peace and You.

Throughout All Life

Children fashioned from ignorance
Sojourn from corruptible things.
No arrogancy escapes smooth lips,
That speak no more exceedingly proud,
For the wicked are silent in darkness
As over the face of the whole earth
They crawl and are cut down accordingly.
Come search through testified sufferings
Follow revealed happiness in things
Received without blemish or spot,
Diligently keep jealousy and anger
From kindling spirit and strife.
Be not weary of correction and truth
For God will guide throughout all life.

Eyes

With my eyes I touch your gentle face
Your soft sweet eyes shall mine caress
And taste the fragrance of your smile.
You whom I love deep in my soul
My faith fullness and steadfast love
Shall cover you with a warm glow.
When your impish eyes look into mine
Passion spills and waves or'flow,
You kiss the tears of salt.
Tenderly your hand takes mine
You lead us to the life we seek
Close together for all time.

Tiny Babe

A sense of cosmic loneliness
is swept aside
by a smile of a
tiny baby.
a great grandson
with laughing blue eyes
and puckered mouth.
He lifts the heavy heart
of one gazing upon his
exquisite being, so small,
so fragile, so dependant
upon the family
he'll come to love
as they already
love him who can
animate bubbles
from formula warm
and sweet that tumbles from those pink puckered
lips that one wants
to kiss.

Mystery of Life

Time becomes a capricious dimension
    All too magical for belief,
Reflecting tenderness, excitement, love
    With the sensation of emptiness.
An intangible atmosphere of hope
    Infinite and incredibly devious,
Like the watching of the sea,
    Has a haunting sense of sadness.
Time appears balanced precariously,
    To wait and be forever with fear,
Reflecting for the moment a forgotten anxiety,
    Spontaneously alert in sharp intensity,
Clear and visible consequences condescend
    Known as pleasant to contemplate,
Merely a matter of increasing interest
    In the transfused world mystery.

It's Amazing

It's amazing that the sun comes up
    each and every morn.
It's amazing that the leaves of trees
    rustle, shake are shorn.
It's amazing that clouds so light
    float across the sky.
It's amazing birds fly south
    before the winter's cry.
It's amazing how a babe is born
    then grows into adult.
It's amazing to watch fishes swim
    around, then in then out.
It's amazing how a cat can smile
    and gaze into your eyes.
It's amazing how a ship can float
    amid the ocean's size.
It's amazing that all shadows creep
    among each object glide.
It's amazing how the pot will boil
    when heat is aptly 'plied.
It's amazing how the flowers grow
    with colors deep and true.
It's amazing how a child can smile
    as its toys become unglued.
It's amazing how true friendships last
    with memories of the distant past.
It's amazing how with arms outstretched
    they hold a love to last.
It's amazing how each heart can beat
    To keep the rhythm true.
It's amazing that a friend was found
    When I met you.

In Front of My Window

In front of my window over the sink,
Never a worry or care is distinct.
As He enters my thoughts deep within,
There's impressionable beauty from Him.
At a private showing for me to behold,
Seed in a feeder sparrows enfold.
Against the spacious blue of sky,
Gentle breezes brush on by.
Aged limbs that stretch and yawn
Bluets and buttercups carpet the lawn.
Chipmunks scamper atop the stone wall
Jonquils, poppies, tulips grow tall,
Spring is in front of my eyes as I think
In front of my window over the sink.

Tread It Down

Mountains and heritage are laid waste,
For dragons of the wilderness become
Impoverished with wickedness they despise.
Fires are kindled for naught,
Contemptible with weariness and dreadful
Iniquity not found in the lips unless
Walked in peace and equity and turned away.
Do not cause any to stumble at the law
Deal treacherously with every man but
Profane not for abomination is committed
By all in evil and untruth' so regard not
But goodwill and above all love.
Take heed of the residue of evil against truth,
Cover violence with compassion and delight.
Be a swift witness against oppressors,
For there's no room for them here.
Rebuke and devour evil to destroy it.
Be not vain nor walk mournfully,
Be happy and proud in goodness, truth, love.
Discern between right and wicked,
Burn not in the oven of stubble, instead
Tread it down dreadfully.

Reach Out

My blood is red, my heart is, too!
That's why I reach my hand to you.
I need your help to do the trick
Of turning work to joy – that quick.
My eyes are blue, the vet is, too!
That's why I turn and look to you.
My strength alone is not enough
To serve my God and country's tough.
My heart can bleed, so can yours.
So let's join forces, ease the chores.
My help I give with love true blue,
For community, state, nation and you.

Affliction

Turn with affliction and smite
The waves of the sea,
Dry up the rivers of hatred,
Weep and howl for your miseries
That shall come upon you.
Your riches are corrupted from rust,
Fire will consume heaped up treasure.
Wait for the nourished heart.
Patience received in affliction which
Fell under tender pity and passion
Lay aside all malice and guile.
With well-doing one may force silence
On ignorant foolish behavior
For ability overcomes sadness.

The Burden

How long shall I cry and none shall hear?
Why as I've shown iniquity and grievance?
Spoiling and violence are with me
As are strife and contention.
Bitterness and haste are terrible and dreadful.
Destiny and judgment proceed swift and fierce
To the captive of violence.
Scoff and scorn shall deride the unlawful
Offend not the power of truth and obedience.
Establish correction and purity,
Deal harshly with treachery, devour the wicked.
Be glad at the dragging of evil and continual emptiness.
Enlarge the desire for uprightness,
Heap the taunting with woe and vex the spoilers.
Defy violence with fear and loathing.

Legends of Miracles

With incarnate conscience
        Traditions clustered
                Yet never attains,
Heroic moral stature
        Glad and marveling
                Escape the ambush.
Life is inexplicable with
        Contradiction, swift discernments
                Outbursts of joy.
Legends of miracles loom larger
        Embellishments are wrought
                In auguries of victory.

Only a Rose

As I looked at her I could see
A woman of rare classic beauty.
Snow white hair drawn loosely back
Delicate hands folded gently on her lap.
Unquenchable spirit clearly shown
On softest face where a smile did bloom.
A woman of foresight and thrift
Who seldom a temper would lift.
Could sew a torrentuous storm
Play piano from night through to morn.
Then work in her garden free from weeds
To pick vegetables for canning or freeze.
Gaiety, dancing and books galore
Were her pastime in years before,
Generous sharing of her heart
She gave to people before they'd depart.
Her beauty within glowed right on through,
Aged well over sixty she still went to school.
Her Bible and God treasured she most
As queenly bearing and spirit would boost
Others to overpower their disintegration
When troubles and sorrows did take concentration.
Stern and severe when occasion arose
Mother certainly deserved more than only a rose.

My Dad

He has compassion, my dad,
No cloud can overshadow him.
When he looks round about
Straightway I behold his love.
Amazing strength do I see
For his arms reach out to me.

Saved

The most remarkable thing about life today
Is knowing our Savior is on His way.
Some glorious night, or will it be day?
Jesus will call us all home to stay.
God in His heaven holds out His hand
Beckoning sinners to a much richer land
Filled with angelic singing, prayer and praise
Telling the world how Jesus Christ saves.

Chasing the Wind

Down-to-earth is the everyday concern of
Men and women who are crippling nature.
Working hard to succeed is like chasing the wind
In a tree-starved land that's traumatically trapped.
Time never stands still so to be idle is evil
For carefulness commands creative hands.
Repair the green corridors then unique scenic sites
Emerge among the water-flow of spoils
Propitious euphoria can petrify under perpetual
Permissiveness, decaying the countryside.
Instead infringe upon the detriment of filth
By planting trees, or bulbs or bush in silt.
Bird feeders draw the natural joys of sight
And raking leaves, so pungent, smell just right.
Golden yellow daffodils nodding in the spring
Cover barren ground to forfeit nudity.
Things are brought to their best by struggle
Against harmful babbling problems of life.

No Rejoice

The filthy and polluted obey not,
Receive not corruption and trust.
Unjust know no shame of darkness,
Desolation and waste pass unnoticed,
Corrupt doings dwell aplenty, yet go unpunished.
Prey determined to devour with fierce anger,
Jealousy consents unashamed to evil.
Afflicted have no rejoice in deceit.
None shall slack the sorrow for there is
No fame in the captivity of such assembled evil.

When He Looked Round

When he looked round about on them
Softness of his eyes spread out,
His hands stretched forth in peace
As they told him of their love.
A smile crept over quiet lips
Green specks sparkled in brown eyes,
As he did take heed to hear
The words sown from their hearts.
The cares of past were gone
Choked with emotion galore,
Metered out with unabandon
For the father they adore.

All Ways

Opalescent rain of life
        swept you all ways,
Interminable time in
        brittle, constant obsession,
Kept own fantasies on
        a false note of assurance.
Accumulated irresistible friendships
        filled with solitude shifted,
Without expression a quiet
        acceptance thinned and lengthened,
Rigid and immutable persistence
        impulsively cast interference.
Lostness that lay exposed
        escaped benign tolerance,
As malignant revenge moved
        mercifully to mystic depths,
Uneasiness faded so wraithlike
        in cloudless splendor.

Hearing

Thank you God, for my new life
For helping me combat world strife,
Now I'm quite able to carry on
Knowing you're here from dusk to dawn.
My world has long been silent and dull
Not hearing birds sing in air that's full.
Wind blowing, trains roaring I could feel
Never could hear the sound of bell's peal.
It's noisy now this world I'm in
Has there always been this constant din?
The country sounds I love the most
But thank you God, the perfect Host.

Luscious Springtime

Bursting warmth from flaming sun.
Heats the tight curled shoots,
Then luscious springtime odors run
Free from tip to dampened roots.
Birds chirp sweetly to their Maker
To cast rain from the sky,
While flickering wings they've dusted
From the softened dirt close by.

Height of Hope

Enormously relieved as
        thoughts of escape
                predictable, haunted, repelled
an uninhibited optimism
        of surprising strength
                impatiently, ineffectually struggles
in the irretraceable
        encounter – fragmentary, forlorn
                innocent and lost –
lying languidly in
        luxury, sharp strangulating
                pain deliberately outrageously
stimulates a maze
        of appalling uncertainty,
                as nebulous ecstasy
of hope cautiously
        still, is persuaded
                to pursue the
illusion of youth
        contentedly, curiously calm
                with rich reward.

Rushing Waves

As the waves roared in so close
        to the rocky shore
Music of the water rushing
        overflowed the shore
While the sweeping snatching gulls
        screamed and called for more.
White foam frothed o're slimy weeds,
        catching rainbows from the sun,
Washing out again to spill
        into troubled waters spun
Circling back the waves roared in
        smashing once again for fun.

Toward Tomorrow

Plunging imagination of a
    waking dream
Strode through everything in
    vague disquiet.
Imperceptible shadow of innate
    sensitiveness shatters
Vestigial emotion slipping
    the loneliness.
Undeviating faith sparked a
    spurious thrill
Life crept comparatively relaxed
    toward tomorrow.

Shadows

Under the ancient oak tree
      while the sun crosses the sky,
Shadows creep unnoticed
      by any human eye.
The day of joy has vanished
      as clouds as black as night
Burst forth in rain and hail
      shattering everything in sight.
Grumbling and boastful ramblings
      caress a wicked world,
Dubious truths thrust toward
      all burning hearts turned cold.
Rest in the shade of the oak tree
      on a disquieting day,
Walk with a friend or neighbor
      talk world troubles away.

Why?

As a ship passing through
        billowing water sinks,
As a song flying through
        sound diminishes,
As lightning streaks through
        deep darkness follows,
As wind whips through
        destruction descends?
As wisdom seeps through
        bright radiance abounds,
As understanding slides through
        true graciousness appears,
As faith bursts through
        soft happiness begins,
As love leaps through
        life ascends.

Son Shines

Who sacrificed His life for ours
raised up the trees and, too, the flowers?
Who demonstrates for us each day
a love so powerful we can't repay?
Who will never forget our needs
though His heart so often bleeds?
Do we care that God looks in
the heart of us so crushed with sin?
Do we hope He only sees
the beauty of our too few deeds?
Do we pray God's sacrifice
truly will give us new life?
God's Son shines down on us today!
hurrah, three alleluia's say!!!

Through Dense Darkness

The sound of crunching pebbles
    twisted, cracked and broken,
Blotted out delicately etched gulls
    wheeling gracefully overhead,
Soft moist wind fanned
    across tanned cheeks,
As unseeing tear filled eyes
    stared far beyond,
Through dense darkness.
Wrenching doubts assailed
    through tunnel vision,
Colored mist of fantasy
    curiously manipulating
Unuttered sadness of intimate
    moments of spiritual exaltation,
Mingled involuntarily with
    lacerated soul of despair,
Through dense darkness.
Feeble thoughts flickered
    with deliberate vagueness,
As ripening mind bravely
    crawled objectively inward,
Saturated with quiet
    curiously overtaken by great
Sharp breaths of certitude;
    struggled securely upward,
Through dense darkness.

A Tear is Shed

The road dipped slowly under the car
        on the icy road as though to
Stop the thoughts of having
        to leave the ones so loved.
Just to have more time to share
        the dreams which had once
Seemed so lost but now could
        truly cause a tear to shed.
If only the falling drifting snow
        could cover up the thoughts
Of every darkened dream which
        swirled so thickly through the tears.
There is the sun at last so bright
        the road has finally reached the end
To show the loved as we watch
        on the steps, smiling as a tear is shed.

Feeling Great

Briskly striding around the lake
    feeling incredibly tall and great.
In the doleful drone of the dragonflies
    somber clouds clip across blue skies.
Clear water ripples and splashes the shore
    children with sailboats and laughter galore.
Warm breezes waft the golden beams
    Streaking the sun in shimmering streams.
Diadem of beauty bursts everywhere
    trees and bushes no longer bare.
Summer has sprung so gracefully
    across this land so lovely and free.
Nothing can banish this feeling because
    the pigeon coos and the black crow caws.
As I briskly stride around the lake
    feeling incredibly tall and great.

Life Has Not Lost Its Music

The wraithlike figure smiles broadly,
    Without expression, shifted slightly,
        Look of uneasiness faded.
In mystic depth of quiet acceptance,
    A shadow of discontent dissolved,
        Drew out most secret thoughts.
Irresistible friendliness impulsively escaped,
    Intrigue and interested countenance
        With flourishes of feisty courage stayed.
Difficult to capture and describe,
    Impetuous, persistent politeness displayed
        Through gentle laughing eyes.
Rustic voice resumed its melody,
    As resplendent face with radiant glow,
        Expressed the music of the heart.
Warmth, understanding and tender compassion,
    Song of peace echoing above,
        Stoical simplicity of love,
Life has not lost its music, not at all!
    Just listen rapturously, dear friend,
        You too will hear the glorious call.

The Daughters of the King

T ender is the love we share while
H appiness overflows with care
E ntwining in never ending prayer.

D oing the things we hold most dear
A nd giving others a bit of cheer.
U nmistakable friendships we shall claim.
G athering each other in uplifting laughter,
H astening to build most grateful thoughts
T hat stretch our ever doubtful hearts.
E verlasting friendships flowing in love
R eflecting true spiritual purpose of will
S haring our gladness, courage and still

O ffering ourselves without exception
F orever faithful to do God's will.

T hankful minds give grateful service
H earts that mingle with smiling face
E ternally have God's peace and grace.

K ingdom on earth is God's desire
I n love and obedience we aspire
N ow with refreshing steadfast praise
G od and His Son our spirits will raise.

In the Cookie Jar

Swift rippling laughter
      filled me with delight,
Unbidden images crept
      As children might,
In the cookie jar.
Among the wonders
      of the world today,
Just about everything
      children will say
In the cookie jar.
A choice of kinds
      but never empty
It doesn't matter
      just have plenty,
In the cookie jar.
With desperate glance
      cast over lands,
Children shriek with joy
      and dash dirty hands
In the cookie jar.

Mouth tender and happy
        swallowing hard
Suddenly plunged in despair,
        at finding a card,
In the cookie jar.
No more! No more!
        in colorful tone,
Said the short note
        attached to a bone,
In the cookie jar.
But Mother relented
        shopped and brought home
Many more cookies
        to exchange the bone,
In the cookie jar.

Troubled Waters

Inward rush of troubled waters
    deposit gritty flecked foam high
        as waves roll in unceasing
            splashing mist in noisy rhyme.
Desperate search for freedom finds
    almost unendurable dullness
        when lack of hope defeats
            the spirit of the mind.
To sooth tremendous turmoil
    as disastrous days float past
        caressing clouds in bluest skies
            lurch backward just in time.
Engulfed by sweeter memories
    wrenching doubts assailed
        burning happiness becomes
            bent upon mankind.
Outward rush of troubled waters
    ricochet and flee
        As love rolls gently inward
            the quickened heart to bind.

Sister

Who but you would know
        The need I have for family
To soothe tremendous turmoil
        I feel as my life passes,
Amid this world so thoroughly
        Discouraged and confused?
Who but you would see
        From windows clearly visualize
The brightness of my world outside;
        Caressing clouds in bluest skies
Growing grass in tree-flecked fields
        Gifts from God?
Who but you would hear
        The passing snow drop upon
Bursting buds as spring sounds
        Swallow every echo of the past
To make the future path full
        Of tenderness and love?
Who but you would feel
        Strength from healing hands
Show perseverance, wisdom,
        Understanding of God's fortitude
Where no depth on earth can hide
        Fortress of fond memories?

It Can't Be Bought

Bluest sky
        whitest cloud
                golden sunlight
                        baby's smile,
Soft moist breeze
        the brightest moon
                balm of kindness
                        love that's true,
Misty sea
        foggy hill
                darkest night
                        coldest chill,
A violent temper
        patience of Job
                gentle heart beat
                        falling white snow,
Twinkling stars
        wind in the leaves
                an arched rainbow
                        brisk blown breeze,
Happy dreams
        worthy soul
                bountiful grace
                        loving God.
An idea born
        Lasting friendships
                Ruby red sun
                        Steady rainfall.
Twinkling stars
        Wind in the leaves
                An arched rainbow
                        Brisk blown breeze.

Last Lunge

With bared feet toeing the velvet sand
She sat on a lone white iron seat
Amid the spraying waves of salt,
Paint brush and easel at arm's reach,
In her mind's eye sea gulls were sailing
        In a cotton candy sky
        To dive into the foaming sea
        Disappear and die.
Scanning the heavens blue she saw
Four screaming, swaying fish-catchers make
Their last lunge into the bottomless depth.
Her heart was sad as waves gently quaked
To wash away the ghastly vision,
        Sweep back again and fill
        Clam holes on the beach –
        Become perplexed, then still.
No sharp shells sticking in the sand
To glitter in the spanking sun,
No three-toed markings to criss-cross
The widely wind-blown dune.
No scavengers to partake of treasured food.
No long thin legs
        To tread upon the
        Dirt strewn water's edge.
Why should so mild mannered a mind
Think of annihilation amidst the joy
Of fighting, flying feathered friends,
Pecking here and there, not to destroy
But to keep company with the
        Driftwood and slimy weeds
        That slipped unnoticed
        From the thrashing seas.

That Sinking Feeling!

Give, ear to my words,
        Heed to my groans,
                Hard to the sound as
                        Broken heart bleeds.
That sinking feeling!
A child was born to
        A family of three,
               He lived only days
                      Then God took him away.
That sinking feeling!
Child grown to manhood
      Soon on his own,
            Visits so seldom
                    Then there's a war on.
That sinking feeling!
Bright sunny skies shine
        On garden in flower,
               Clouds black as night burst
                      As hail and rain pour.
That sinking feeling!

The boastful stand round
        In bountiful numbers
                Destroying all truths
                        With rigorous lies.
That sinking feeling!
Be gracious and kind to
        Neighbors, sounds hollow,
                Rambling and inconsequential
                        Put off till tomorrow.
That sinking feeling!

Joy

Momentarily
shaken by
>angry words of
>in deniable pride yet equally
>torn in feelings and belief,

Fear
of rueful
>countenance blink and
>terrific loneliness tend to
>pierce a weak and vanished soul.

Flourishes
of love
>and laughter lightly
>take away the thorns
>to build bubbling buoyant joy.

Friendship

F reedom in the heart when found
R eaches out to touch a friend,
I nward rush of troubled waters
E ngulf the lost and lonely soul,
N o way can sadness overcome
D estroyed by true love of a friend,
S weetness amid sorrow's lost music
H elps hold head high with honor,
I n the pure strong hour of the morning
P eace comes from the trust of a friend.

Narrow the distance
Yet fast the clock.
Pleasant the memories
As we depart.
    . . . .
Chances are we'll
Meet again.
Way up yonder
With our Heavenly Father.